DON'T BELIEVE EVERYTHING YOU THINK

*Why Your Thinking Is the
Beginning & End of Suffering*

JOSEPH NGUYEN

Don't Believe Everything You Think

© 2022 One Satori LLC | ISBN: 9798427063852

First printing edition 2022 in the United States

For Kenna,

an angel on earth who taught me what unconditional
love truly is and how it can change the world

TABLE OF CONTENTS

WHAT YOU WILL DISCOVER IN THIS BOOK & HOW TO GET THE MOST OUT OF READING IT

This book was written to help you find everything you've been searching for and the answers to all the questions you've had your entire life. I understand this is a bold statement, but you will shortly see why I have complete confidence in saying this.

What I know to be the truth from the depths of my soul is that you will not be the same person you were after reading this book. The only constant is change. Growth is an inevitable process of life, and it will be impossible for you not to change after reading this book.

"We cannot change what we are not aware of, and once we are aware, we cannot help but change." - Sheryl Sandberg

No matter who you are, where you're from, what your background is, what you've done and haven't done, what status or wealth you do or don't have, Martian or not, you can find total peace, unconditional love, complete fulfillment, and an abundance of joy in your life. I promise you are not the exception, even though it may seem like it. Love knows no boundaries. An open mind and a willing heart are all you need to receive every answer you've been looking for.

And yes, there are extremely practical implications and byproducts of understanding what is inside of this book, which many of my coaching clients have experienced, such as a 2-5x increase in income, exponential growth in their businesses, deeper and more harmonious relationships, overcoming lifelong addictions, the spontaneous disappearance of destructive habits, an increase in health, vitality, and overall energy. Miracles like these occur daily for many who understand the principles within this book. And this is just the tip of the iceberg. If I were to list some of the improvements and results people have gotten from this understanding, more than half of this book would be stories of such daily miracles.

I am reluctant to mention any of these "external" results because it is not the point of this book. These physical manifestations are the byproduct of this inside-out understanding of how our experiences of life work. In actuality, we only want external results like money and significance because we want to experience certain feelings inside, such as love, joy, peace, and fulfillment. The feeling is really what we want in our lives, not the physical things, but the trap is that we believe the physical things will give us those feelings. The secret lies within the feeling.

This book will help guide you to uncover the truth you already know within and discover these feelings you've been looking for your entire life.

Don't read this book for information. Read it for insight. Insight (or wisdom) can only be found within. That is why it is called insight (in-side). To find everything you're looking for in life, you must look inside yourself and discover the wisdom that already exists within you. All the answers lie deep within your soul. This book is merely a guide to help you look in the right place. I truly admire anyone who still has the hope that what they're looking for is still out there. This means you have hope. Without hope, we have nothing, so the fact that you're here, reading this now, is a testament to your faith, courage, and strength. I know with one hundred percent certainty that you will find what you're looking for if you continue down the path you're on with the hope you have in your heart.

I want to make it clear that this book is not the only book that contains truth. The truth lies within everyone and in everything. You must look beyond the form (the physical) to see and experience the truth (the spiritual). The words in this book are not truth. They point TO the truth.

Look beyond words to see the truth for yourself. Truth cannot be intellectualized; it can only be experienced. The truth lies within a feeling, which is why it cannot be formulated into a word.

If you want to find truth, look beyond the words and **look for a feeling**.

Many who discover the truth describe the feeling as complete peace, unconditional love, and overwhelming joy. People also describe it as the most familiar, unfamiliar feeling. It feels like you're finally home. Look for that feeling, and everything will be revealed to you. In this book, I will not say anything you don't already know deep inside your soul. This is why it will be a familiar, unfamiliar feeling when you experience the truth.

Don't try to use your intellect to figure it out — you won't. As soon as you intellectualize it, you've missed it. The truth does not come from memorizing a sentence or two. A child can do that, but they will not understand the truth. The truth comes in the form of a feeling. From that feeling will come the wisdom and truth you seek, which will set you free. That's what we're all ultimately seeking, isn't it?

What I will unveil to you in this book will seem simple. It will seem almost too simple, and your brain (ego) will try to fight it or attempt to make it more complex. It will think that it can't be this simple. When that time comes, I want you to remember that the truth is always simple. What is complex can always be broken down into its smaller counterparts. The truth cannot be broken down into smaller constituents, which is what makes it truth. This is why truth is always simple. **If you want to find the truth, look for simplicity.**

Approach this book with an open mind and a heart of pure intention to know the truth, and you'll receive everything you've been searching for.

Before we move on, I want to express my deepest gratitude for you being here and sharing your time and attention with me. Those are some of the most valuable life forces you could give to another, so thank you for that gift to me, which you are also giving to yourself. Never forget your own divinity because it is only through our divinity that we have our humanity.

With Love & Light,
Joseph

CHAPTER 1

THE JOURNEY TO DISCOVERING THE ROOT CAUSE OF SUFFERING

"People have a hard time letting go of their suffering. Out of a fear of the unknown, they prefer suffering that is familiar." — Thich Nhat Hanh

There is an important distinction to make when speaking about suffering. When I mention suffering in this book, I'm referring to psychological and emotional suffering. There is a way in which, no matter what happens in your life, you do not have to suffer emotionally and psychologically.

I am not saying what we go through is all in our heads or made up. Terrible and unfortunate events happen to people every single day. I'm saying that although we experience a lot of pain in our lives, suffering is optional. In other words, pain is unavoidable, but how we react to the events and circumstances that happen in our lives is up to us, and that will dictate whether we suffer or not.

Buddhists say that two arrows fly our way whenever we experience a negative event. Being physically struck by an arrow is painful. Being struck by a second emotional arrow is even more painful (suffering).

The Buddha explained, "In life, we can't always control the first arrow. However, the second arrow is our reaction to the first. The second arrow is optional."

When I first heard of this quote from Buddha a few years back, I was confounded because although I understood what he meant, I didn't know how I could apply this in my own life. If anyone were given the clear choice of suffering and not suffering, I don't think anyone in their right mind would choose to suffer.

How can I choose not to suffer? If it were as easy as that, I don't think anyone would suffer anymore. It wasn't until years later that I came across a new understanding of where suffering comes from that I could stop it at its source.

As I began my journey of self-improvement, I came across many different teachings, studies, and methods to help people overcome their problems. I read dozens, if not hundreds of books, studied psychology, went to therapists, listened to many different thought leaders, tried changing my habits, waking up at 4 am, changing my diet, becoming more structured and disciplined, shadow work, studying personality types, meditating daily, going on spiritual retreats, following spiritual masters, and researching different ancient religions.

If you name it, I've probably tried it. I was desperate to find an answer because I wanted to know how to stop suffering in my own life and help others do the same. Although some of these things did help me improve incrementally, it didn't stop my suffering. I still always felt highly anxious, fearful, unfulfilled, irritated, angry, and frustrated every day. Even after doing all of that, I still didn't discover the answer, and, if I'm being honest, I was even more lost than before I started on this quest.

I felt purposeless, hopeless, and directionless. I didn't know what to do anymore, where to look, or who to talk to. It wasn't until I was in my darkest hour that a glimmer of hope began to lead me to the light.

All of a sudden, after years and years of searching, I stumbled upon one of my first mentors who revealed the answer to how I could alleviate my suffering.

The answer I discovered was in understanding how our minds work and how the human experience is created.

CHAPTER 2

THE ROOT CAUSE OF SUFFERING

"One who looks around him is intelligent; one who looks within him is wise." — Matshona Dhliwayo

We live in a world of thought, not reality. Sydney Banks once said, "Thought is not reality, yet it is through thought that our realities are created." Each of us lives through our own perceptions of the world, which are vastly different from the person right next to us. An example of this is that you could be sitting in a coffee shop having a quarter-life existential crisis, completely stressed out of your mind about how you have no idea what you're doing with your life when it seems like everyone else has theirs together, while the person next to you is happily enjoying their freshly brewed drink while peacefully people watching. You are both in the same coffee shop, smelling the same aroma, surrounded by the same strangers, but how the world looks to both of you couldn't be more different. Many of us go through the same events or are in the exact location at the same time, yet are having completely different experiences of the world.

Here's another example of how we live in a world of thought and not reality. If you walk up to 100 different people and ask each of them what money means to them, how many different answers do you think you'll get? Close to 100 different answers!

Money is technically the same thing, but it means something different to each person. Money could mean time, freedom, opportunity, security, and peace of mind, or it could mean evil, greed, and the reason why people commit crimes. For now, I'm not going to get into which one is right or wrong (hint: there is no right or wrong answer, but that's for a different chapter).

Another illustration of this concept is as follows: If you survey 100 different people and ask each of them what they think of our current president, how many different answers do you think you'll get?

Even though it is the same person we're talking about, we will get 100 different answers because most people live in their own thoughts and perceptions of the world. The meaning (or thinking) we give an event determines how we ultimately feel about it. That meaning or thinking is the filter through which we see life from then on — because of this, we live through a perception of reality, not in reality itself.

Reality is that the event happened with no meaning, thinking, or interpretation of it.

Any meaning or thinking we give the event is on us; that is how our perception of reality is created. This is how our experience of life is created from the inside out.

It's not about the events that happen in our lives, but our interpretation of them, which causes us to feel good or bad about something. This is how people in third world countries can be happier than people in first world countries, and people in first world countries can be more miserable than people in third world countries.

Our feelings do not come from external events, but from our own thinking about the events. Therefore, we can only ever feel what we are thinking.

Let's hypothetically say that you really hate your job, and it causes you an enormous amount of stress, anxiety, and frustration. It pains you even to set foot in the building where you work, and just thinking about your job makes you furious. When you're thinking about your job, you're just sitting on a sofa with your family, watching a TV show together, but you are fuming at the thought of your job. Everyone else is having a good time except you.

At this moment, everyone else in your family is having a different experience of life than you, even though the same event is happening. Just the thought of work created a whole different perception of reality, even though you're not physically at work.

If it were true that external events cause us to feel the way we feel inside, then you should be a happy camper in your living room, watching a funny TV show with your family every single time you do this activity — but that's not the case.

Now, you may be saying that you're only feeling this way because an external event, your job, is causing you to feel stressed and anxious. To that, I'll ask the question, is it absolutely true that every single person feels the exact same way about the job they're working in?

Two different people can be doing the same job but will have completely different experiences. It can be the most amazing experience and a dream job for one person but be another person's worst nightmare and living hell. The only difference between one person and the other is how they think about their job, which determines how they ultimately feel about it.

Let's return to your original scenario of hypothetically hating your job. Remember how much stress, anxiety, and frustration it causes you when you think about it?

Let's do a quick thought experiment about that by answering the question below:

Who would you be without the thought that you hated your job?

Take 1 minute to see what comes up for you, and don't move on until you do that.

If you don't overthink it and truly let the answers surface from within you, without that thought, you will most likely feel and be *happy, peaceful, free, and light.*

Without our usual thinking about a particular event or thing, our experience of it completely alters. This is how we live in a world of thought, not reality, and how our perception of reality is created from the inside out through our own thinking. With this new understanding, you've just uncovered the cause of all our human psychological suffering...

The root cause of our suffering is our own thinking.

Before you throw this book across the room and light it on fire, I'm not saying that this is all in our heads and isn't real. Our *perception of reality* is very real. We will feel what we think, and our feelings are real. That is completely undeniable. However, our thinking will look like an inevitable, unchangeable reality until we begin seeing how our reality is created. If we know that we can only ever feel what we are thinking, then we can change our feelings by changing our thinking. Thus, we can change our experience of life by knowing that it comes from our own thinking. And if that is true, then we are ever only one thought away from experiencing something different and transforming our entire lives at any moment — through a state of no thought.

In short, the moment we stop thinking is when our happiness begins.

A Young Monk & the Empty Boat (A Zen Story About How Thinking is the Cause of Our Own Suffering)

A long time ago, a young Zen monk lived in a small monastery in a forest near a small lake. A few senior monks occupied the monastery, while the rest were newcomers and still had much to learn. The monks had many obligations in the monastery, but one of the most important ones was their daily routine, where they had to sit down, close their eyes, and meditate in silence for hours at a time.

After each meditation, they had to report their progress to their mentor. The young monk had difficulty staying focused during his meditation practice for various reasons, which made him very mad. After the young monk reported his progress to his mentor, the elder monk asked a simple question with a hidden lesson, "Do you know what is really making you angry?" The young monk replied, "Well, usually, as soon as I close my eyes and meditate, someone is moving around, and I can't focus. I get agitated that someone is disturbing me even though they know that I'm meditating. How can they not be more considerate? And then, when I close my eyes again and try to focus, a cat or a small animal might brush past and disturb me again. By this point, even when the wind blows and the tree branches make noise, I get angry. If that is not enough, the birds keep on chirping, and I can't seem to find any peace in this place."

The elder monk simply pointed out to his pupil, "I see that you become angrier with each interruption you encounter. This is exactly the opposite of what the point of your task is when meditating. You should find a way not to get angry with people, animals, or anything around you that disturbs you during your task." After their consultation, the young monk went out of the monastery and looked around to find a place that would be quieter so that he could meditate peacefully. He found such a place at the shore of the lake that is nearby. He brought his mat, sat down, and started meditating. But soon, a flock of birds splashed down in the lake near where the monk was meditating. Hearing their noise, the monk opened his eyes to see what was happening.

Although the bank of the lake was quieter than the monastery, things would still disturb his peace, and he got angry again. Even though he didn't find the peace he was looking for, he kept returning to the lake. Then one day, the monk saw a boat tied at the end of a small pier. And right then an idea hit him, "Why don't I take the boat, row it down to the middle of the lake and meditate there? In the middle of the lake, there will be nothing to disturb me!" He rowed the boat to the middle of the lake and started meditating.

As he had expected, there was nothing in the middle of the lake to disturb him, and he was able to meditate the whole day. At the end of the day, he returned to the monastery. This continued for a few days, and the monk was thrilled that he had finally found a place to meditate in peace. He didn't feel angry and could calmly continue the meditation practice.

On the third day, the monk sat in the boat, rowed to the middle of the lake, and started meditating again. A few minutes later, he heard water splashing and felt the boat was rocking. He started getting upset that even in the middle of the lake, someone or something was disturbing him.

Opening his eyes, he saw a boat heading straight towards him. He shouted, "Steer your boat away, or you will hit my boat." But the other boat kept coming directly at him and was just a few feet away. He yelled again, but nothing changed, and so the incoming boat hit the monk's boat. Now, he was furious. He screamed, "Who are you, and why have you hit my boat in the middle of this vast lake?" There was no answer. This made the young monk even angrier.

He stood up to see who was in the other boat, and to his surprise, *he found no one in the boat.*

The boat had probably drifted along in the breeze and had bumped into the monk's boat. The monk found his anger dissipating. It was just an empty boat! There was no one to get angry at!

At that moment, he remembered his mentor's question, "Do you know what is really making you angry?" And then wondered, "It's not other people, situations, or circumstances. It's not the empty boat, but my reaction to it that causes my anger. All the people or situations that make me upset and angry are like the empty boat. They don't have the power to make me angry without my own reaction."

The monk then rowed the boat back to the shore. He returned to the monastery and started meditating along with the other monks. There were still noises and disturbances, but the monk treated them as the "empty boat" and continued meditating peacefully. When the elder monk saw the difference, he said to the young monk, "I see that you have found what is really making you angry and overcome that."

CHAPTER 3

WHY DO WE THINK?

"I think and think and think, I've thought myself out
of happiness one million times, but never once into it."
— Jonathan Safran Foer

As humans, we have evolved to develop a sophisticated ability to rationalize, analyze, and think because it simply helps us survive. Our minds do an incredible job of keeping us alive, but it does not allow us to thrive. It is concerned solely with our safety and survival, not fulfillment or joy.

The mind's job is to alert us of potential dangers in our environment that may threaten our lives. It does its job so well that not only will it scan our immediate surroundings for threats, but it will even reference our backlog of past experiences to create hypothetical scenarios and predict what it thinks could be future potential dangers based on our memories.

None of this is wrong by any means. The mind is simply doing what it was designed to do. When we don't understand that its only duty is to help us survive, then we will get angry and frustrated with it. All conflict is derived from an innocent misunderstanding. Our mind's duty is to keep us alive. Our consciousness's duty is to help us feel fulfilled. Your soul is the reason why you're even on this journey in the first place — to find peace, love, and joy for yourself.

Your mind has done an amazing job at what it was made to do, but now you may relieve it of its job because we no longer live in the wild where death could be right around the corner in a bush. If we keep using our minds, we will constantly stay in a state of fight or flight, anxiety, fear, frustration, depression, anger, resentment, and all negative emotions because the mind thinks everything is a threat to our very existence. If you want to be free, happy, peaceful, and full of love, then you will need to let go of listening only to your mind and go beyond it by tuning into something much greater that will help you not just to survive, but to thrive.

CHAPTER 4

THOUGHTS VS. THINKING

"Stop thinking and end your problems." — Lao Tzu

Thoughts are the energetic, mental raw materials we use to create everything in the world. It's important to know that thoughts are a noun and aren't something that we *do*, but something we have. A thought takes no effort or force on our end, and it is something that just happens. We also cannot control what thoughts pop into our minds. The source of thoughts comes from something beyond our minds — the Universe, if you will.

Thinking, on the other hand, is the act of thinking about our thoughts. This takes a significant amount of energy, effort, and willpower (which is a finite resource). Thinking is actively engaging with the thoughts in your mind. You don't have to engage with each thought in your mind, but when you do, that is thinking.

Thinking is the root cause of all our psychological suffering.

Now, you might wonder, where do positive thoughts fit into the picture? Positive thoughts, or thoughts that feel good do not result from thinking. They are, instead, generated by our natural state of peace, love, and joy. They are a byproduct of a state of being, not a state of thinking. We will go into depth about this in the next chapter.

For now, let's do a quick thought experiment.

I'll ask you a question, and all you need to do is be aware of what you're experiencing, and we'll review what happened afterward.

What is the dream amount of money you want to make in a year?

Pause here and wait for an answer to surface.

Give yourself about 30-60 seconds to think about your answer to how much money you want to make in a year.

Don't move on to the next step until you've had a decently sized train of thought about how much you want to make.

Now, take that amount and multiply that by 5.

What do you think about this new dream goal for your income when we multiply it by 5?

Take at least another 30-60 seconds to become aware of your feelings when you think about them and see what other thinking comes up for you as you feel your emotions.

Don't move on until you've done the above.

Okay, let's bring it back in and review what happened.

After I asked the first question about the dream amount of money you want to make per year, an answer popped into your mind within a few seconds. That is a thought. Notice how quickly and effortlessly that came to you.

After an answer popped into your mind, I asked you to think about your answer. What happened once I asked you to think about your answer?

If you're like most people, you probably went on a wild rollercoaster once you began thinking about the thought.

You might have been thinking how there's no way you can make that much, no one in your family is making that much money, you don't know how to make that much, it's stupid to want that much money or that it makes you greedy.

Notice how you felt when you were thinking about those thoughts.

Most likely, it didn't feel that great, but that is okay, and I'll show you what you can do about it soon.

This is a prime example of thoughts versus thinking.

If I ask you a question, you will 100% have a thought that pops into your mind.

Thoughts are not inherently bad. They are intrinsically neutral. The moment we think about our thoughts is when we begin to get taken on an emotional rollercoaster. When we think about our thoughts, we begin to judge and criticize the thoughts and experience all sorts of internal emotional turmoil.

When I asked you how much you wanted to make, you had a thought about the amount. That thought was neutral and didn't cause any emotional toil. You might have felt expansive and excited. It was only when you began thinking about that thought of how much you wanted to make, which is what caused the self-doubt, unworthiness, anxiety, anger, guilt, or any other emotion you may have experienced.

This is what I mean by thinking is the root of our suffering. The initial thought of how much you wanted to make didn't cause any suffering until you began *thinking* about the thought of how much you wanted to make.

It is not necessary to think about our thoughts or to judge them. It does us no good to do so. We may think that thinking is helping us, but all it's doing is causing us to feel all these negative, unwanted emotions and making us create reasons why we can't do it or why we shouldn't want it.

The only useful and helpful thing was the initial thought that popped into your mind when I first asked how much you wanted to make. All of the thinking that happened after was destructive and unhelpful.

Thoughts create. Thinking destroys.

The reason thinking destroys is because as soon as we begin to think about the thoughts, we cast our own limiting beliefs, judgments, criticisms, programming, and conditioning onto the thought, thinking of infinite reasons as to why we can't do it and why we can't have it.

Without thinking, we prevent all negative programming and judgments from tarnishing the initial thought of what you want to create.

If I asked you what are some ways you could make the amount of money you want, if you sat there long enough, you'll experience the same phenomenon of having random thoughts pop into your head of ways you could make it happen.

These are thoughts of creation. Thoughts have the qualities of being infinite and expansive and feel energetically aligned with you. You'll know you have thoughts from the divine when you feel positive emotions, lighter and alive.

As soon as you begin thinking about those thoughts of the ways you can make the money you want, you'll immediately feel heavy, restricted, and limited, along with a whole onslaught of negative emotions. This is how you'll know if you're thinking.

I use my feelings as an internal radar that tells me whether I'm getting direct downloads of thoughts from the Universe or if I'm in my head thinking about my thoughts.

You can only ever feel what you're thinking, so feelings and emotions are like an intuitive internal dashboard that tells me if I'm overthinking.

If I have many negative emotions, I know I'm thinking too much. This is another example of how we're naturally built for success.

On the next page is a chart that compares Thinking vs. Thoughts to help you identify which one is which within your mind. It is helpful to go through a few examples of thoughts in your mind and using the chart to identify if it is an actual thought or if it is thinking.

Thoughts vs. Thinking Chart

Attribute	Thought	Thinking
Source	Universe	Ego
Charge	Neutral	Negative
Weight	Light	Heavy
Energy	Expansive	Restrictive
Nature	Infinite	Limited
Quality	Creative	Destructive
Essence	Divine	Mortal
Feeling	Alive	Stressful
Emotion	Love	Fear
Sense	Wholeness	Separateness
Effort	Effortless	Laborious
Root	Truth	Illusion
Time	Present	Past/Future

CHAPTER 5

IF WE CAN ONLY FEEL WHAT WE'RE THINKING, DON'T WE NEED TO THINK POSITIVELY?

"We are ever only one thought away
from peace, love, and joy — which come from a
state of no thought." — Dicken Bettinger

There is a caveat I haven't mentioned yet to the principle that we can only feel what we're thinking. The more accurate way of describing it is that we can only ever feel negative emotions when we are thinking.

The goal isn't necessarily to completely stop feeling negative emotions. Some negative emotions can be helpful, such as feeling fearful when walking down a dark alley alone with no one else in sight.

These negative emotions are only helpful for survival, but if we don't constantly encounter life-or-death situations, negative emotions are more unhelpful than helpful for most of us.

We're going to be moving forward with the context that we're not struggling for physical survival, so we'll be using the context that negative emotions are not necessary most of the time.

When I mention that we can only ever feel what we're thinking, most people assume we must think positively to feel positive emotions.

Instead of convincing you if this is true, let's do another thought experiment so you can experience the truth for yourself.

Recall a time when you felt the most joy and love you've ever felt in your life, and feel the feelings you felt as much as you can for at least 30 seconds.

What thoughts were going through your mind at that peak moment when you felt the most joy and love? (I'm not asking what you were doing at the time, but what thoughts were going through your head at that exact moment.)

Many people who answer this realize they had no thoughts during that exact moment. For others, they say that the thought was that they were so grateful or happy.

For those who answered that they had the thought that they were grateful, did you feel that joy and love before you had that thought or after?

Take 10-15 seconds to answer that question before moving on.

What insights and epiphanies did you have?

What's surprising is that most people didn't have any or many thoughts going through their mind when they felt the happiest and the most amount of love in their lives. Those who had the thought that they were grateful felt that way **before** having that thought.

If they had that thought, it happened after they felt the feelings, so the thought could not have produced the emotion.

This brings us to another truth: **you do not have to have thoughts or think to feel positive emotions.**

The beautiful part about truth is that it needs no justification because it can be experienced right here, right now. It doesn't need to be proven or rationalized to you, and you experienced this truth firsthand by the experiment we just did.

Here's why we don't need to have thoughts or think to feel positive emotions like joy and love.

Our natural state of being IS joy, love, ecstasy, freedom, and gratitude. This may be hard to believe because if it's natural, why don't we always feel that way? I'll answer this in a bit.

If we want to see the natural state of anything, one of the best ways is to look at nature and its state in its infancy (before it is affected and conditioned by its environment).

For example, let's look at the natural state of a baby. What is a baby's natural and default state (assuming the baby wasn't abused, neglected, or had any physical issues)? Are babies naturally stressed, anxious, fearful, and self-conscious? Or are they naturally in a state of bliss, happiness, and love?

Our natural state of being is joy, love, and peace. Therefore, any thinking we do will only take us away from those natural states of being, which is why whenever we feel highly stressed, we have a LOT of thinking going on. The strength of the negative emotion we feel is directly proportional to how much thinking we are doing at the moment.

On the other hand, the intensity of the positive emotion we feel is inversely proportional to the amount of thinking we are doing at the moment. In other words, the less thinking we have going on, the stronger the positive emotion we feel in the present.

To see the truth in this, recall a few other memories when you were highly stressed and anxious and see how much thinking was going on then.

Take about 1-2 minutes to do this.

Then, recall a few memories where you were at your happiest or felt the most joy and love and see how much thinking you had going on at that time.

Take another 1-2 minutes to do this before moving on to really experience and internalize the truth of what you see.

My mentor taught me an analogy that helped crystallize this concept: imagine our mind has a speedometer (like in a car), but instead of miles per hour, it is thoughts per minute. The more thinking we have going on, the higher the "thought-o-meter" goes, and if we have enough thinking going on, it'll go into the red zone. This is when we feel incredibly stressed, burned out, frustrated, and angry.

It is not the content of our thinking that causes us stress, but that we are thinking, period. The amount of thinking we have going on is directly correlated to the magnitude of stress and negative emotions we are experiencing at any given moment. When you're experiencing a lot of frustration, stress, anxiety, or any negative emotions, know that it is because you're thinking. The intensity of those emotions is directly correlated to how much thinking is going on.

Therefore, it's not WHAT we're thinking about that is causing us suffering, but THAT we are thinking.

To summarize, we do not have to try to "think positively" to experience love, joy, bliss, and any positive emotions we want because it is our natural state to feel those emotions. The only times we don't naturally feel these emotions is when we begin to think about the thoughts we're having, thus blocking the direct connection to Infinite Intelligence, and we feel stressed, anxious, depressed, and fearful. It is not about the content of our thinking, but that we're thinking, which is the root cause of our suffering. The intensity of the negative emotions is directly correlated to the amount of thinking we have going on in the present. The less thinking we have, the more space we create for positive emotions to naturally surface.

CHAPTER 6

HOW THE HUMAN EXPERIENCE IS CREATED - THE THREE PRINCIPLES

"If the only thing people learned was not to
be afraid of their experience, that alone would
change the world." — Sydney Banks

At its fundamental level, the human experience is created by these three principles: Universal Mind, Consciousness, and Thought. These three principles work together to allow us to experience everything we do in life; if one of the three is missing, we won't be able to experience anything. Sydney Banks first discovered these principles, and now I have the humbling privilege of sharing them with you.

Understanding these three principles enables us to know how we can alleviate ourselves from our suffering, but also allows us to create from Source.

Universal Mind

Universal Mind is the Intelligence behind all living things. It is the life force and energy that is in all things. It is how an acorn knows how to grow into a tree, how the planets know how to stay in orbit, and how our bodies know how to heal itself when we get a cut. It's how our bodies know how to self-regulate and keep us alive without us having to manually do everything, like breathing and beating our hearts. The Intelligence that knows how to do all this and is in everything is called the Universal Mind. Many call this God, Infinite Intelligence, the Quantum Field, Source, and other names. This is where Thoughts come from and everything else in the Universe. All things are connected by Universal Mind. There is no separation between anything, and any time there seems to be separation between things, it is merely an illusion of our thinking. When we are connected to Universal Mind, we feel whole, fulfilled, filled with love, joy, peace, and inspiration. It is only when we begin thinking (believing the illusion or ego) that we block this flow of Universal Mind and begin to feel separated, frustrated, lonely, angry, resentful, sad, depressed, and fearful.

Universal Consciousness

Universal Consciousness is the collective consciousness of all things. It is what allows us to be aware that we exist and aware of our thoughts. Without Universal Consciousness, we wouldn't be able to experience anything. Our five senses would be useless because there's nothing to be aware of. This is what brings things to life and makes them perceivable to us.

Universal Thought

Universal Thought is the raw material of the Universe from which we can create from.

It's the object we can perceive through Consciousness. Without Thought, we would have nothing to be aware of. Thought is like the DVD that contains all the information for us to watch the movie on the TV. The TV and DVD player are like Consciousness — they allow us to have a mechanism to bring the information on the DVD to life so we can watch and experience the movie. The electricity needed to power the DVD player and TV is like Universal Mind in the sense that it is the invisible energy/force that connects and powers all things. It is the Source from which everything can work and function.

CHAPTER 7

IF THINKING IS THE ROOT CAUSE OF SUFFERING, HOW DO WE STOP THINKING?

"A crowded mind leaves no space for a peaceful heart."
— Christine Evangelou

Heaven and Hell: A Zen Parable

A tough, brawny samurai once approached a Zen master deep in meditation. Impatient and discourteous, the samurai demanded in his husky voice so accustomed to forceful yelling, "Tell me the nature of heaven and hell."

The Zen master opened his eyes, looked the samurai in the face, and replied with a certain scorn, "Why should I answer to a shabby, disgusting, despondent slob like you? A worm like you, do you think I should tell you anything? I can't stand you. Get out of my sight. I have no time for silly questions."

The samurai could not bear these insults. Consumed by rage, he drew his sword and raised it to sever the master's head at once.

Looking straight into the samurai's eyes, the Zen master tenderly declared, "That's hell."

The samurai froze. He immediately understood that anger had him in its grip. His mind had just created his own hell — one filled with resentment, hatred, self-defense, and fury. He realized that he was so deep in his torment that he was ready to kill somebody.

The samurai's eyes filled with tears. Setting his sword aside, he put his palms together and obsequiously bowed in gratitude for this insight.

The Zen master gently acknowledged with a delicate smile, "And that's heaven."

It's not possible to just entirely stop thinking, but we can reduce the time we spend thinking so that it gets smaller and smaller each day that passes. Eventually, we can get to the point where we spend most of our day not caught up in our thinking and live in a blissful state most of the time.

When we say that we want to stop thinking, many people assume that we are trying to stop all thoughts in general. This isn't what we're trying to do. Now that you know the difference between thoughts and thinking, we are working on allowing thoughts to come and flow through us while we minimize the thinking about those thoughts that emerge.

The most interesting and almost paradoxical thing about stopping our thinking is that we don't have to do anything to minimize it other than to be aware of it. By us becoming aware that we are thinking and that it is the root cause of all our suffering, it automatically makes us conscious to that fact and we become detached to it, allowing it to settle and pass. This takes almost no effort and is done through pure presence in the moment.

Here's an analogy from one of my mentors that illustrates this concept:

Imagine I give you a bowl of cloudy, dirty, murky water. If I asked you, how you would make the water clear, how would you do it?

Take 15 seconds to see what answers you come up with before moving on.

Most people say something like filtering the water or even boiling it. What most people don't realize is that if we let the bowl of dirty water sit for a period of time, we can see that the dirt begins to settle on its own in the water, and after a while, the water becomes clear on its own.

This is how our minds also work. If we let our thinking sit without disturbing it by trying to "filter" or "boil" it, the thinking will settle down on its own, and our minds will become free from thinking. The natural state of water is clear, and the natural state of our minds is also clear if we do not disturb it.

If life begins to feel unclear, disorganized, and stressful, and you're not sure what to do next, you now know that it's only because your thinking is stirring up the dirt, making your mind cloudy and difficult to see ahead. You can use this as an indicator to help you realize you're thinking too much.

Once we become aware of the fact that we are only feeling what we're thinking and that thinking is the root cause of our unpleasant experience, we see it for what it truly is. Then, we allow it to settle by giving it space, and slowly, we will see how we begin to have a clear mind again.

You can also compare thinking to quicksand. The more we fight our thinking, the more it amplifies negative emotions and worsens them. The same is true for quicksand. If we're in quicksand, the way out isn't to fight it. If we panic and frantically try to fight it, it only makes things worse by tightening the grip it has on us and pulling us under faster. The only way out is to stop struggling and allow your body's natural buoyancy to take over to bring you back to the surface easily. The only way to break free from our thinking is to let go and trust that our natural inner wisdom will guide us back to clarity and peace like it always has.

If you find yourself fluctuating between thinking and non-thinking, know that it is completely okay and quite normal. There is no way that we can remain in a state of non-thinking every second of every day, and if we try to make that a goal, we will cause ourselves to suffer by forcing ourselves back into thinking again.

We are spiritual, infinite beings having a physical, finite experience. Because of this, we are a living gateway between the human and the divine, so we will naturally oscillate between the two states of feeling anxious/stressed and joyful/peaceful. We cannot control or prevent the oscillation between thinking and non-thinking, but we can minimize the time spent thinking and, thus, create more moments where we feel joyful, peaceful, passionate, and full of love.

Although not being able to control when we begin to think can seem like we are cursed with an inevitable fate, it is not something to worry about because we can always return to the state of non-thinking. It is just a part of our beautiful human experience.

What can give us true peace is knowing that we always have this state of pure peace, love, and fulfillment underneath any thinking that we may ever have at any given moment. That beautiful state we always want is something we can never lose, but only forget. But just because we can forget it doesn't mean it's not there. Just like when it becomes night and the sun sets, we know the sun is always there; we just can't see it. If we think when the sun sets that it may never come back, then understandably, we will have a lot of anxious and fearful thoughts. The same is true for our state of being.

We are ever only one moment away from remembering that we always have that infinite well of clarity, love, joy, peace, and fulfillment. We will forget sometimes, but when we do remember and realize that we are caught up in our thinking when we experience negative emotions, that alone will allow us to return home to our natural, beautiful state. All we have to do is remember it, know that this is just our thinking, and have peace knowing that the sun is not gone forever and will rise again soon enough. Having that understanding will also allow us to appreciate the nighttime for its existence and role in the universe. From that, we can see how it is meant to be a part of our human experience and begin to cherish its beauty as much as the sun.

CHAPTER 8

HOW CAN WE POSSIBLY THRIVE IN THE WORLD WITHOUT THINKING?

"Anxiety is thought without control.

Flow is control without thought." — James Clear

Here's a question that will guide you to an insight about this question:

What thoughts are going through your head when you're doing your absolute best work where you're fully captivated and entranced by what you're doing at the moment?

Take about 15 seconds to wait for an answer to pop up before moving on.

If you still haven't had the insight or epiphany from the answer, here's another question that may point you in the right direction:

When you love what you do so much and are completely engrossed in it that you lose all sense of time and space (aka when you're in a state of complete flow), what thoughts are going through your mind as you're in the state of flow at the moment?

Pause here and wait for the answer to arise (give it about 30-60 seconds for the insight to come in).

When you are doing your best work and are in a total state of flow, where there is no separation between you and the work you are doing, you have no thoughts. And if you have thoughts, they're flowing right through you without you having to think about them. In other words, the state of peak performance for humans can be described as the state of non-thinking. It may seem crazy, but we do our best work when we aren't thinking, and you just proved it with your own experience.

Here's another example that will help illuminate the truth of this topic. When professional or even Olympic athletes are competing, do you think they are thinking and overanalyzing every single thing that's happening during the game? How much thinking do you think is going on during the competition for them? The highest-performing athletes will describe when they are in their peak state that they are in "the zone." This "zone" is the state of flow or non-thinking.

In Japanese culture, they have a beautiful word to describe this phenomenon: mushin.

Here is the definition from Shotokantimes:

"Mushin is achieved when [the] mind is free of random thoughts, free of anger, free of fear, and particularly free of ego. It applies during combat and or other facets of life. When mushin is achieved during combat, there is an absence of loose or rambling thoughts. It leaves the practitioner free to act and react without hesitation. He reacts according to all the study and training that has brought the karateka to this point. Relying on, not what you think should be your next move, but on what your trained, instinctive, subconscious reaction directs you to do."

After practice, thinking hinders the performance of athletes, and the same is true for everyone. We only hesitate, are reluctant, have doubts, insecurities, and fears only when we begin thinking and over-analyzing. We function, perform our best, and embody our full potential when we enter a non-thinking state. Without thinking, we are free from the limitations of the ego and can create the most incredible things in the world. I am not asking you to adopt this belief but to try it and experience it for yourself so that you gain the insight to make it your own.

CHAPTER 9

IF WE STOP THINKING, WHAT DO WE DO ABOUT OUR GOALS, DREAMS & AMBITIONS?

"There are no limitations to the mind except those we acknowledge." — Napoleon Hill

I think, therefore I suffer.

When I finally understood that thinking was the root cause of my suffering, I was jumping up and down, exhilarated, relieved, and grateful for discovering the true reason for everything negative I've experienced. This ecstasy was short-lived though because soon after the exuberance settled, the following thoughts popped into my mind:

If thinking is the root cause of all my suffering and I stop thinking, how do I live my life now? What about all of my goals, dreams, and ambitions? Do I stop wanting things in life? Will I devolve into a couch potato and not do anything with my life anymore?

In case you were wondering, yes, I am telepathic and yes, I can read your mind. I'm just kidding, but if you are wondering how I wrote the exact or very similar questions and know what thoughts you most likely have right now, it's because I am also human, contrary to popular belief. All of us are going through similar journeys of awakening to our True Selves, so rest assured that many people are having the same thoughts you are having right now as you come to see your true magnificence.

Now, back to what we do about our goals, dreams, and ambitions if we stop thinking. As I pondered these questions, an incredible amount of fear and anxiety began to surface because I thought that I would have to give all of it up and become a monk in the middle of the mountains.

I was not ready to do that. As much as I wish I were that enlightened and detached from my life, I genuinely enjoyed being in the world, experiencing the fullness of life with other people, even if a large portion of my life was filled with suffering.

Here's what I've discovered about what to do with our goals and dreams with this new understanding. As we've mentioned in previous chapters, there's a difference between thoughts versus thinking. The source of thoughts and the source of thinking are different, and the source is what will dictate whether it causes suffering or not.

Similarly, where our goals and dreams come from will determine whether we feel great about pursuing them. Like everything in this world, there is nothing inherently good or bad; only our thinking makes it so. Goals, dreams, and ambitions are not good or bad, so it's not an either-or situation, but more about where those goals come from.

There are two sources of goals: goals created out of inspiration and goals created out of desperation.

When goals are created out of desperation, we feel an immense sense of scarcity and urgency. It feels heavy, like a burden, we may even feel daunted by the colossal task we've just committed ourselves to, imposter syndrome and self-doubt begin to manifest, and we always feel like we never have enough time for anything. We go about our lives frantically, desperately searching for answers and ways to accomplish our goals faster, always looking externally, never feeling enough or that we can ever get enough. Worst of all, if we achieve our goal, within a few hours or days afterward, all those feelings of lack begin to resurface. We start not feeling content with what we have done, unable to savor our accomplishments, and because what we did never feels like it's enough, we feel that same way about ourselves. Not knowing what else to do, we look around for guidance externally to see what others are doing and see they're continuing to do the same thing. Thus, we proceed to set another goal out of desperation in an attempt to escape all of the negative feelings gnawing away at our souls. When we dig a little deeper into these types of goals we set, they are all typically "means goals" and not "end goals." In other words, the goals we set in this desperation are all a means to an end. There's always a reason we want to accomplish the goal, and it's always for something else. For example, we want to create a multi-million-dollar business because we want financial freedom or to quit our jobs to escape the stress and anxiety that comes from it. We feel like we HAVE to do these things instead of WANT to. Goals created from desperation are typically "realistic" and created from analyzing our past and what we think to be "plausible" at the moment. It feels very confining and limiting. Although these goals and dreams may excite us in the moment, as soon as we begin to try to create them, we feel a lack and are desperate to bring the dream to life. Paradoxically, if we achieve a goal created out of desperation, we end up feeling even more empty than before. The next "logical" thing we tend to do is to set an even bigger goal out of even greater desperation to hopefully make us feel whole inside.

This is how most of us set our goals and live our lives. I'm also not saying this to criticize or judge at all, but to reveal the reality of it. The only reason I could describe it in excruciating detail was because that was my life.

Here's the good news: it's not your fault you set goals that way if you are, and there's a way out. It's through creating goals and dreams out of inspiration instead of desperation.

When we create goals out of inspiration versus desperation, it is an entirely different story. In this state, we are creating because we feel deeply moved, inspired, and expansive. It feels like a calling rather than an obligation. It is like a powerful force of life is coming from within us, wanting to be expressed through us to be manifested into the physical world. This is why painters paint, dancers dance, writers write, and singers sing, even if they never get paid or make a living from it. We feel pulled by a force to create something. We gravitate towards it. We feel compelled to do it. When we feel like this, we create from a place of abundance instead of lack.

Most surprising is that in this state, we are creating not for any reason other than simply wanting to. We don't create because we feel like we HAVE to. We create because we want to, and there's no other reason. We aren't creating these goals so that we can do something else or use it as a means to get something else we want. This type of creation comes from a place of wholeness and abundance. It's an overflowing of love and joy for life. This is the reason why most of us want or have kids. It's not so that we can milk our kids for their money once they're old enough to work and use them as a retirement plan. We want to have kids because we want to share the abundance of what we have with them, and it comes from a place of sharing what we have lots of versus trying to get something out of them.

This feeling of deep inspiration is incredibly difficult to describe because it does not come from this world. It doesn't come from us, but through us from something greater than us. I like to call this feeling divine inspiration because our ideas and vision of what we want to create seem far bigger than we could have imagined or come up with ourselves. Since divine inspiration doesn't come from us but from something greater, it doesn't analyze or rely on past data or what you or anyone else has already accomplished. Divine inspiration happens when groundbreaking inventions are created that seemed impossible not too long ago. It knows no boundaries, limits, or constraints. It is an expansive force that energizes and lifts us, making us feel "high" on life. In this state, we feel whole, complete, and filled with unconditional love, joy, and peace. We don't analyze, compare, criticize, judge, or rationalize anything, but instead, we truly live, love, share, give, create, grow, and nourish. It is one of the greatest feelings we can experience, and it is truly a gift that we can experience the divine as humans (and it's because we're from the same source).

Everyone has experienced this deep feeling and desire to create something marvelous in the world out of pure inspiration and not desperation. Before moving on to the next paragraph, I encourage you to test this theory. Pause here and spend a few minutes thinking about times in your life when you felt an overwhelming feeling and desire to create something magnificent because you felt deeply inspired and called to. It doesn't matter if you actually created it or not, but think of a time when you felt that feeling to create out of inspiration.

Isn't that just one of the most amazing feelings in the entire world? Most of us feel this divine inspiration, but then suppress it as soon as we begin thinking about doing it. We begin to think ourselves into doubt, rationalize why we can't do it, tell ourselves that it is unrealistic, how we should focus on more important things, and that we're not good enough to do it. As soon as we begin to think about the thought of wanting to create, it completely shuts off the source of that inspiration, and we go back to living life as usual. When we cut off that source, we also cut off the feelings of abundance, vitality, ecstasy, joy, and pure unconditional love and go back to the feelings of doubt, anxiety, frustration, sadness, and feel confined, stuck, and frustrated with our lives.

We can only ever follow one calling at a time, either inspiration or desperation in the present moment. The two cannot coexist simultaneously, but we can fluctuate between the two depending on how much thinking is going on.

When we stop thinking, we don't stop having goals and dreams; we fall back into our true nature and create goals and dreams out of inspiration versus desperation. We begin to allow thoughts from the Universe to come into our mind, leading us to divine inspiration to create something that has never been created before. Following divine inspiration makes us feel alive, whole, joyful, love, peace, and fulfillment.

So, how can we tell when a goal or dream is created out of inspiration or desperation?

A simple way to know if a goal or dream is created out of inspiration is to remember the distinction between thoughts and thinking. Goals and dreams that come in the form of thought are created out of inspiration. Goals and dreams that come from thinking are created out of desperation.

Typically, when we think, we'll analyze, judge, criticize, rationalize, and use our past to create our new goals, but this form of creating goals feels restricting and limiting. We don't typically feel good when creating these types of goals, and when we're pursuing them, we do not feel great either since it's all out of desperation.

Another way to identify the two is to sense how you feel energetically. Goals and dreams created out of desperation will feel heavy, draining, confining, and empty. We tend to feel a lot of scarcity, fear, and stress like we HAVE to do it or are obligated to. With these types of goals, it seems like if we do not accomplish them, there will be dire consequences, hence the high pressure and stakes. I'm sure you can see now how this can create a feeling of desperation.

Moreover, we're trying to accomplish these goals to escape our current situation and get out of something. Our goals created in this state are typically means goals, meaning that we want to achieve these goals so that we can do something else afterwards, such as having the goal to quit our job. Most likely, you'll have this goal because you want to do something you actually enjoy, but you can see how the goal of quitting your job is just a means goal for you to do something else. Or having a goal of making $1 million is typically set because you want financial freedom and travel the world. These goals are always a means to an end, not the end itself. There's always a reason that we want to accomplish these goals, and it makes us feel very empty inside.

I want to emphasize that none of these goals are inherently wrong or that we shouldn't have goals of wanting to make money or quitting our jobs. If those goals are created from inspiration, that is entirely different. It just depends on the source of the goals and not necessarily the goal itself. This is an important distinction to make, otherwise you'll spend most of your time debating and stressing yourself out over if this is the right goal for you or not. There is no right or wrong goal, only goals created from inspiration or desperation. It just depends on how you want to feel inside, and when you're aware of these two types of goals and how they manifest, you'll be able to feel blissful as you create amazing things in your life.

On the other hand, goals and dreams created out of inspiration (which comes from thought) feel very light, energizing, uplifting, and expansive. We tend to feel excited, joyful, and, most importantly, inspired. We don't feel like we HAVE to create it, but that we WANT to. Instead of feeling like you NEED to do this, you feel inspired to. There is virtually no pressure because we're not trying to get out of something or escape our current situation by accomplishing this goal. There is no scarcity or urgency because we don't feel like we're creating from a place of lack, but instead from a place of abundance and just want to share it with the world. Since it's coming from inspiration, we are not doing it to get something out of it so that we can do something else. It's not a means goal, but simply an end in and of itself. There is no "reason" we need to create it. We are not creating to feel whole, but because we feel whole and want to give from that place, not expecting anything from it.

I'm sure you can see the stark difference between the two now and that you can tell which type your goals currently fall under. If most of your goals fall under desperation, don't worry because most people have goals created from desperation, including myself, before I knew a better way.

So how do we create goals and dreams out of inspiration versus desperation?

Creating goals and dreams from divine inspiration isn't something you have to try to do. We naturally have thoughts of infinite inspiration all the time. If you look at children, they naturally have the wildest dreams and imaginations of what they want to do. It almost doesn't even register in their minds that they can't do something most of the time. The only difference between us and children is that we have learned to shut down all these thoughts of inspiration, which contain our dreams, hopes, and goals that we genuinely want to see manifested in the world. Our minds are filled more with reasons of why we can't than thoughts of what we want to create.

We innately have an infinite flow of inspiration that comes through us, but we block that flow as soon as we begin thinking about our thoughts, which causes self-doubt, self-sabotage, and anxiety. Think of the flow of inspiration to create like a river. The river always flows until man puts something there to block it, like a dam. Then, when the dam is there, we ask why there are so many fish dying, animals disappearing, and forests dwindling when all we need to do is return the river to its natural state, and everything will be working perfectly fine, the way nature intended it to.

This is the same for our minds and our goals. We always dream, have big goals, and know what to do when we're tapped into our intuition, free from thinking. If we do not think about our thoughts, any thoughts about dreams, goals, and desires that naturally arise are all from the divine, and that is how you "create" goals out of inspiration versus desperation.

A question that significantly helps me to settle the thinking and tap into the limitless well of possibilities of what I could create is:

"If I had infinite money, already traveled the world, had no fear, and didn't receive any recognition for what I do, what would I do or create?"

Whenever we ask questions, answers *always* arise. It is impossible for our brains to hear a question and not come up with a response. So when you ask yourself this question, whatever begins to come up for you without any manual thinking will be from the divine and inspiration versus desperation.

The way the question is worded is critical because it removes most of the thinking, fear, criticism, and external reasons why you would want to do something, so it focuses your answer on what you genuinely want to create (usually, it's for no reason other than you just wanting to create it because it's fun), without any influences from the material world.

Try asking the question and seeing what comes up for you! You'll be surprised at what surfaces, but don't get caught up with your thinking when your true dreams begin to be revealed to you.

To a mind without the limits of thinking, anything is possible.

CHAPTER 10

UNCONDITIONAL LOVE & CREATION

"The greatest power that mankind could ever achieve is the power of unconditional love. This is when people love with no limitations, conditions, or boundaries." — Tony Green

Unconditional Love

I learned unconditional love from my extraordinary partner, Makenna. For most of my life, I always questioned everything. I had to know the reason why things were the way they were. Otherwise, I would go crazy. I couldn't just experience life without knowing the meaning and reasoning behind everything.

Naturally, as anyone would in a relationship after dating for about a year, I asked Makenna why she loved me. She innocently replied that she didn't know why; she just knew she did. Then she asked me why I loved her, and I listed dozens of different reasons why. It ranged from her beautiful smile to her adorable laugh, how pure her heart is, how much she loves her family, how intelligent she is, and the list goes on almost indefinitely.

We dated for seven years before we got married, and every few months after that first time I asked, I would ask her why she loved me, and even up until this point, she still says the same thing, "I don't know, I just know that I love you — a lot."

This slightly bothered me for so long because I didn't understand why she didn't know why she loved me. I could list 50 reasons why I loved her, but she couldn't list a few. Throughout the years, I still loved her so much that I didn't mind that she didn't know. I just accepted it and continued loving her anyway because I couldn't help myself.

It wasn't until a few months ago that it dawned on me why she couldn't think of why she loved me. I began to question the reasons that I had for why I loved Makenna. Then, I had an epiphany that changed my life forever.

I asked myself, did I love her because of her laugh or because she loves helping other people? What happens if she doesn't laugh one day or doesn't help someone that day? Do I stop loving her if she doesn't do the things I said were why I love her? I realized that if I create reasons for why I love her, then it makes my love for her conditional to those specific traits or actions, and if she doesn't do them, then I don't love her. This is, of course, not true.

At that moment, I had the awe-inspiring insight that Makenna couldn't list reasons why she loved me because her love for me was unconditional. There were no reasons why she loved me; if she had reasons, it would mean she only loved me if I were exuding those traits or doing those things she had in her mind.

Her love for me is not based on my mood or what I did; her love for me goes beyond all "reasons" and does not come from a place of reciprocity. She does not love me because I love her, nor is she loving me because of what I can do for her. She is experiencing so much love within herself that it's an outpour of an abundance of love that she is gifting me unconditionally.

Attempting to articulate the feeling of this and where it comes from is probably the hardest thing I've ever done in my life because I'm attempting to describe the indescribable.

From this experience, I learned to make my love for Makenna unconditional by not placing reasons or conditions for when I would love her (because if I did that, by default, I would put conditions on when I would not love her). There is just so much love in me now because I've experienced it. There is simply an outpour of unconditional love where I can't help but love her no matter what. This unconditional love doesn't come from external reasons, but from within from the infinite source we all came from.

We are all connected to this pure, unconditional love, which is God, the Universe, or whichever name you choose to use. The only thing that gets in the way of this is our own thinking, which separates us from that unconditional love.

Unconditional Creation

Unconditional creation is the purest form of creation there is. When something is created from unconditional love, we can't help but stand there and admire it in awe. Unconditional creation is always innovative, unique, new, captivating, bold, different, and revolutionary in its own way. Very few people operate in this space because we always put conditions around what we do or make.

For example, whenever we are working to achieve the goal of making more money, we might try to create income for ourselves. This is conditional creation because no one wants money just to have money. Most people want money for something else or to be able to use it for another thing they want.

This, by nature, makes what they are creating conditional. They are only creating this because they want something else out of it. When we create something for something else, typically, we do not enjoy the process of creating because it is always just a means to an end, never an end in itself.

This is why we always feel like we're chasing, grinding, hustling, trying, and constantly stressed and overwhelmed. Even after we accomplish our goal, we'll only enjoy it for those few seconds, and then we're off to another goal we have to chase because we never actually got what we were looking for.

What we're ultimately looking for are feelings. We want more money to get a sense of security and peace. We want to spend time with our family because it makes us feel so much love and joy. We want to do what we love because it gives us a sense of fulfillment. These are all ultimately feelings that we are trying to get, but we keep thinking that the goal or object we want will give us those feelings. This idea is flawed because our feelings can only be generated from within us, not from external things. External things can prompt us to create the feelings, but ultimately, we produce those feelings from within ourselves.

What's paradoxical (like everything in the duality of life) is that **when we create something without conditions or reasons, we immediately feel all the positive feelings we want.**

Unconditional creation is creating something without it being for another purpose, but purely to create it because we want to create it. It's not for money, fame, love, or anything else. We create it simply because we want to create it. This is creation from abundance. When we create from this state, we already feel whole inside, and all the love we want to feel is what we're feeling in the moment.

We can only pursue unconditional creation if we are in a state of non-thinking. Our brains will make us think it is pointless to do something simply because we want to, but that is the secret. As soon as we do things for no other reason, we step into the realm of living our life unconditionally. This is when we experience flow, oneness, and a direct connection to the Universe/God.

CHAPTER 11

WHAT DO YOU DO NEXT AFTER EXPERIENCING PEACE, JOY, LOVE & FULFILLMENT IN THE PRESENT?

"Don't think. It complicates things. Just feel, and if it feels like home, then follow its path." — R.M. Drake.

If you've been applying the principles in the book, you've most likely been able to find peace through non-thinking. If not, I highly encourage you to remember that all of our negative feelings come from our thinking. All you have to do is become aware of that fact, which will settle the thinking like the debris settling in dirty water. Once you see that it is just your thinking and that there's nothing to be afraid of, you will experience true peace in your life in the present.

Once you have been able to experience peace, you might be unsure as to what to do next. At this point, you may be experiencing worry, anxiety, and doubt. Many people, including myself, wondered if they had lost their edge and drive to do anything. **Don't worry; this is normal and part of the awakening process.**

You've already learned the most challenging part: to practice non-thinking and prevent negative thinking from controlling your life.

We may start to feel worried, anxious, and doubtful after we've experienced peace because we have just let go of everything we thought we knew in the world. What actually happened was the death of the personal ego. A natural consequence is that once the personal ego is threatened, it will do everything in its power to regain control over your life again.

The ego is something we can't quite get rid of forever, which is why even after you experience peace, there may be feelings of doubt, worry, and anxiety. At this moment, the ego (thinking) will resurface to attempt to reclaim your throne. But fear not because you've already learned how you can quickly dismantle your ego (your thinking) by remembering that your thinking is the only cause of your negative feelings. The point is not to try to prevent your thinking from ever entering your mind but to shorten the time it takes to remember that it is just your thinking causing negative emotions. It's impossible to prevent thinking from happening because it's so ingrained in us.

For example, it's in our human nature that when we suddenly see that we're about to step on a venomous snake on our path, we will freak out. But when you realize that it's just a piece of rope, you see through the illusion, knowing that your thinking caused you to become afraid, and you resume your peaceful walk on the beautiful trail. We can't prevent that initial reaction, but we can always remember the truth and return to our natural state of peace — and that's all that matters.

Another reason that we may feel anxiety, worry, and doubt once we experience peace is that we are using a colossal amount of energy when we are thinking all of the time. Most people spend the majority of their day in a state of stress (thinking), which consumes enormous amounts of energy. When we stop thinking, this energy we used to think is now "freed up," but it hasn't been directed anywhere yet, and what happens is we return to our old patterns of putting that energy back into thinking because that is how we were conditioned. What we can do in this case is to channel the newfound energy into our goals of inspiration. This is the cure and intervention of preventing this energy from going back into overthinking.

For this to work, make sure you've spent some time creating your goals out of inspiration (versus desperation) and having it top of mind to channel all of your energy towards it once you experience this phenomenon. If you have only goals of desperation in your mind, then directing energy towards it will only perpetuate the thinking and negative feelings.

What tends to help many people in this stage is also having an "activation ritual." An activation ritual is a morning routine that helps them get into a state of non-thinking and flow. It enables you to build momentum in a positive direction immediately when you wake up so that it's easier to stay in that state of non-thinking for the rest of the day. An object in motion will stay in motion. I never understood why spiritual masters and all great leaders have a morning routine until I understood the power of non-thinking and momentum.

Here's the good news: now that all of your energy isn't tied up into thinking anymore, you can use this freed-up energy and channel it into creating new goals from inspiration to fuel and propel you into your new life full of peace, joy, and love.

CHAPTER 12

NOTHING IS EITHER GOOD OR BAD

"There is nothing either good or bad but thinking makes it so." — William Shakespeare

Here's an analogy that helps put this into perspective. On a piano, there are 88 keys. When we look at a piano, we don't point out specific keys for no reason and say that that key is "wrong." We only think a particular key is "wrong" if we think someone is playing a specific song and hits a key that isn't in the song.

Inherently, the piano has no wrong keys, though. Only keys and notes sound more or less pleasant when played consecutively.

Just like how there are no wrong keys on the piano, there are no "wrong" decisions in life. There's only thinking that gives us pleasant or unpleasant feelings. **Putting things into a bucket of right or wrong, good or bad,** creates duality and conditions in our lives, which determines how we feel.

For instance, if we believe that opposing political parties are wrong or bad, this can cause animosity within us and make us feel a concoction of negative emotions.

If, on the other hand, we see different political parties in the same way as there are different keys on the piano and how there are no inherently "wrong" parties, then we open ourselves up to experience love, joy, and peace in the moment. We begin to see alternative perspectives that we haven't seen before and have an opportunity to deepen our understanding of the true nature of life.

Another example would be hiking on a mountain and stopping at specific points to look at the beautiful view. There are no "wrong" spots that we can stop at, stand in, and take in the magnificence of nature, but by being open to all possible places we can stand in, we can see the view from different vantage points we haven't seen before.

Instead of looking for right or wrong, good or bad in the world, look for truth. Instead of trying to prove we are right and they are wrong, or how they're better and we're worse, look for the truth in what's in front of you. I caution this by saying that many people believe what they think is the truth. For the most part, without this more profound understanding of life, most of what we think is not truth, even though it may seem like it.

The actual truth is not subjective. If it is "true" for one person but not for another, then it is not a universal truth. Look for what is universally true for every conscious human being on the planet, no matter who they are, where they're from, and their background. That is the truth, and where you'll find everything you've been searching for. Remember that the only place you can find this is deep within your being, so don't try to look for it outside of you.

If you're confronted with something that may stir up negative emotions, go within yourself to find the source of universal truth deep within your soul. If you look for the answers outside or dig into external reasons for why you feel this way, you will be looking for the rest of eternity and will never find it.

Negative emotions are an indication of misunderstanding. When negative emotions grip us, it means that we believe what we are thinking. At this moment, we forget where our experience comes from and that our thinking is the cause of our negative emotions.

All you have to do is remember that thinking is the root cause of how we're feeling. Once this is brought to your awareness, don't fight the thinking. Just become aware that your thinking is causing the ill feelings, welcome it with love, and it will slowly dissipate before your eyes. Not too long after, you'll return to your natural state of peace, love, and joy.

CHAPTER 13

HOW DO YOU KNOW WHAT TO DO WITHOUT THINKING?

"The intuitive mind is a sacred gift, and the rational mind is a faithful servant. We have created a society that honors the servant and has forgotten the gift." — Albert Einstein

Although there are no ultimately right or wrong decisions we can make, just like there are no wrong keys on a piano, there are decisions or "keys" that are more aligned with us than others depending on the context. Knowing there is no right or wrong relieves us from the pressure to "choose the right one."

When we make decisions, we want to rely on non-thinking. When we try to think, analyze, create pros and cons lists, and ask everyone (including our pets) for advice, it causes anxiety and frustration until we make the decision. Most of the time, we already know deep down what to do in any specific situation. This is often referred to as your gut feeling, intuition, or inner wisdom. What we do is try to confirm our intuition with the external world, and this is where most of the negative emotions begin to surface, wreaking havoc on our mental state because of everyone's opinions.

Only you can know what you want to do. No one else can tell you this. There will be mentors and coaches who can guide you to help you along the way, but the best ones will tell you to listen to your intuition and look within yourself for the answer (the truth is only ever within you). This is why many of us experience the phenomenon of regret when we knew deep down what we should have done based on our gut feeling, but we ignored it and listened to someone else's advice or opinion.

Your intuition will always lead you to where you need to go and what you should do at any moment. It's like a real-time inner GPS that will tell you when to take a detour and which path you should take if there is a blockage on the road to your destination. It's guaranteed that our inner GPS will guide us to exactly where we want to go, but what's not guaranteed is how or which path it will put us on to take us there. There are infinite circumstances that can happen on the journey to the destination, but you can rest assured your GPS will get you there.

Important Note:

Society will almost never confirm our intuition until it's mainstream already. For this reason, if you try to look outside for confirmation on what you know to be true for you, you'll almost always get backlash and differing opinions on what next steps you should take. Avoid looking externally for answers. Follow your intuition, gut feeling, inner wisdom, and the Universe/God. When you do this, you will begin to see miracles occurring in your life that you never could have expected or even dreamed of. Those with the faith and courage to do this will discover the true joy, peace, and love they have been looking for while enjoying the miracle of life.

So, how do we know what to do without thinking?

The truth is we tend to know what to do, but we are just afraid to do it. For instance, if we want to lose weight, we already have a good idea of what we need to do. The formula for losing weight isn't rocket science or written in hieroglyphics. Most of us know that all we need to do is burn more calories than we consume, work out, eat healthy foods, and we'll lose weight. For anything in life, you most likely already know deep down what to do, but are afraid of doing it or don't believe that you are good enough to do it.

The first step is realizing that you already know what to do, but think you don't because of fear or self-doubt. If you don't have any fear or self-doubt about the situation and still don't know what to do, then the next step is to trust your intuition (Infinite Intelligence) to give you the answers you need. We have the ability to access an infinite number of thoughts, so there's no shortage of ideas on what you can do at any given moment. The only thing stopping us from accessing this abundance of knowledge is our thinking.

Henry Ford once said, "Whether you think you can or can't, you're right." If we walk around our lives thinking we can't, we immediately block ourselves from the limitless possibilities of what we can do. But when we release the brake in our mind and realize that it's just our thinking holding us back, we automatically return to our natural state of abundance and unlimited possibilities, and at that moment, we can receive any answer we need on what to do.

CHAPTER 14

HOW TO FOLLOW YOUR INTUITION

"Have the courage to follow your heart and intuition. They somehow already know what you truly want to become. Everything else is secondary." — Steve Jobs

In a previous chapter, we talked about how we don't need to think to thrive in the world and that we grow most by letting go of the thinking holding us back. Flow is a state of pure oneness and a direct connection to everything around us. Because there is no separation when we are in that state, we can also say that it is a state where we are in direct connection and alignment with God/Universe/Infinite Intelligence.

What thinking does is sever this connection we have with the divine, causing us to feel stress, frustration, anger, resentment, depression, and all of these negative emotions many of us feel daily. This is why some religions describe Hell as a complete separation from God.

For simplicity's sake, I'll be using the term non-thinking instead of flow, but they are synonymous when I use them in this book. This state of non-thinking also means a direct connection to Infinite Intelligence.

Many will attribute the state of non-thinking or flow to a particular activity that we love to do, and that's the only time we can be in flow. This is far from the truth. We can be in a state of non-thinking at any point in time. The only time we can be in a state of non-thinking is in the present moment. We can only see reality in the present moment, and when we are actively thinking, it means we are either in the past or the future (which don't exist). Only in the present moment can the truth be found. This is why all spiritual masters and leaders always teach us to meditate, pray, and be in the present moment. In the Bible, when Moses asks God his name, He replies, "I am." God didn't say He was or will be (because they don't exist), but simply with "I am." God, truth, the Universe, freedom, peace, joy, and love (these terms are all synonymous) can only be found, and therefore experienced, in the present.

When you're following your intuition, it means you are trusting yourself and having faith that you always have the inner wisdom necessary to help guide you through everything in life. This is a state of non-thinking or flow.

Let's explore how we can make this concept practical and bring it into our everyday lives. What does following

your intuition and inner wisdom look like, and how can we do it?

When you're following your intuition, you're entirely tapped into something greater than your personal self. You're in a state of non-thinking (flow) and direct connection with God. In this state, you always know what you need to do without thinking and are guided by Infinite Intelligence. It almost seems like we're not doing anything when we're in this zone because we lose our sense of personal self and become one with life. When we're in this state, miracles occur, such as business deals coming out of nowhere, people showing up at the right place at the right time, money coming in exactly when we need it, connections that we were looking for spontaneously falling upon our laps, and life seems almost magical. Time seems to warp and bend around us, and it's because there is no sense of it. We proceed to accomplish more within a few days than others within a month. Abundance, love, joy, peace, harmony, and gratitude are inevitable and inseparable feelings experienced in this state.

Every single person has experienced instances where they have felt like this before. Although many have experienced this phenomenon, very few can maintain it for extended periods. The main reason is that most relapse into thinking and believe they must "figure it out" themselves. When we begin thinking, we lose the power of creating miracle-like events and circumstances.

We don't have to have it all figured out, nor will we ever have it all figured out. How can our limited minds possibly understand and try to manipulate the entire world to our desires?

It is only when we think we know more than God that we run into problems.

The great news is that we don't have to know more than God or even think. All we have to do is trust in our intuition and have faith that our inner wisdom will show us the best way for us. When you ask people who are the most abundant, joyful, and successful how they made it, they will usually attribute their success to some higher power or luck. These people have trusted in something greater than themselves and thus attribute it to that instead of attributing their success to sheer willpower and brute force.

So much in life is out of our control, and we can only control a very limited portion of it. This is not to say that we give up because we can't control our lives; it's quite the opposite. When we realize that we don't have to control and try to force everything to happen our way, we become free from suffering, pain, and frustration and begin to fall into this state of non-thinking where things just all happen for us instead of to us. We start to see that everything was perfectly placed in our lives to help us become the exact person we are now and that if anything were changed, we would not have what we do now. Millions of circumstances and events must have been meticulously orchestrated for us to be where we are now. To plan that would be impossible and futile, yet here we are. This is the miracle of life.

To go back on a point we just made about us not having to control things in our lives, there's a caveat I want to highlight. We cannot control everything that happens in our lives, but we can control whether we think or not (which is the root cause of all our problems and negative emotions). We can decide to change our experience of life whenever we want and how we feel at any moment. This is how we can choose to be happy — by choosing to let go of our thinking. Isn't that what ultimately matters at the end of the day? It's not about what we have, but how we feel inside that is the true measure of success, joy, and fulfillment.

Although we can't control many things, we can have a say in what we want in our lives, but not necessarily the how. For instance, we have the gift of imagination (access to Infinite Intelligence), which means we can come up with anything that we want in our lives. This is an amazing blessing, but things can go sour when we think we need to figure out "the how" to make it happen. At this point, most people give up or continue down the path of brute force to try to bring it to life and suffer daily for it. This is why people believe we must suffer for what we want. That is not true. It is only true if we think we must figure out the "how" to get what we want. Our job is determining WHAT we want, not how to get it. The how is really up to the Universe. This is the best-case scenario anyway because there are an infinite number of ways to bring about what you want in life, so for our little finite brains to figure it out would be futile, nonetheless.

We only suffer when we try to figure it all out, but we don't have to. This is when we want to rely on our intuition and inner wisdom to help show us exactly what we need to do in real-time to manifest what we want. There's no need to try to figure it all out in advance. **Our part is to hold in our minds what we want and get into a state of non-thinking. This enables us to access our Infinite Intelligence (God) so that the answers are revealed to us exactly when we need them.**

The path forward is only revealed when we begin walking. There's never going to be a time when the entire path is illuminated for us to see beforehand because there are infinite ways our desires can manifest.

We must have complete, unwavering faith that what we want to create will come to us, and we can only do this by fully trusting in the Universe to orchestrate how it will happen. We can always get what we desire in life; it just may be different from our timeline or *how* we want it to manifest.

Our intuition (God) speaks to us all of the time. You know that small voice inside that always *knows* what you should do? Maybe it's to leave your job, forgive someone who hurt you, ask someone out, or reconnect with someone. It's that gut feeling you get where you know what you need to do. Have you ever regretted not doing something in a moment your gut told you to do it? Have you ever had a gut feeling to do something but have no logical reason for doing it anyway, and amazing things happened afterward?

That is your intuition.

Our intuition speaks to us through thoughts, but remember that there's a stark difference between thoughts and thinking, as discussed in a previous chapter. Thoughts are divine by nature, and we feel like they pop into our minds out of nowhere. On the other hand, thinking is the negative judgment of our thoughts, which feels heavy and typically has negative emotions attached. When you have thoughts from Infinite Intelligence, there's a sense of knowingness and alignment. It contains the truth, and you just know deep down that it's right. Your intuition will rarely seem logical or rational, but that's precisely what we want because we don't want it to be predictable. If it were predictable, it wouldn't be miraculous, and it wouldn't contain the infinite possibilities of the Universe, which are all spontaneous by nature.

Your intuition will almost always go against your logical, rational mind, so be prepared. It will whisper to you that you should talk to this random person in a coffee shop, which leads to a beautiful friendship, or that you should call up a friend spontaneously when you find out they need someone to be there for them during a difficult time. It will tell you to step into and live in your divine gift and put yourself out there to share the truth of what you know. It will softly beckon you to pursue what you truly want versus following what everyone else says you should want. These are a few examples of the infinite number of ways it will speak to you, and when you follow it, it will always create miracles and abundance beyond your wildest imagination.

So why don't more people listen to their intuition if it always knows what to do and creates abundance whenever it is followed? Fear.

Listening to our intuition can be daunting. This is because our intuition lives in the space of the unknown. In other words, our intuition is spiritual and operates in the field of infinite possibilities, which by nature is the field of the unknown. Humans always fear the unknown because we can't predict what might happen. Only when we step into the unknown can we begin to experience the limitless possibilities that life can bring us. This is why magical things and miracles happen when we trust our intuition. We are literally stepping into the zone of pure possibility. For this reason, we only need to know the "what" of what we want to manifest, not the "how."

The only way you can enter this space of miracles is through non-thinking. If we think, we immediately get ejected out of this space and enter a state of anxiety, worry, and suffering. Our thinking will try to predict what might happen based on the past. This is why most people get more of the same of what they have always gotten. They try to use their limited personal mind to create something they have never experienced before, innocently not realizing that they must step into the unknown by entering a state of non-thinking and listening to their intuition. We can only ever create something we have never experienced in the realm of infinite possibilities, but the only way to make that happen is to go where we haven't gone before, which is the unknown.

In summary, your intuition always knows what you need to do in the present moment, but the only way to access it is by getting into a state of non-thinking. Your personal mind will freak out because you're stepping into a space of infinite possibilities (the unknown), but if you remember that it is just thinking that is making you feel fear, the fearful thinking will fall away, and the courage you need to act on your intuition will naturally surface. In this moment, you must have faith in your intuition to guide you through life even when you don't know what will happen next — but that's the adventure and joy in it. The unknown is the only way to manifest what you want in life if you don't already have it. You must do what you haven't done to get what you don't have. When you're operating from intuition, it's not like you're going to feel fear all of the time. The fear is only present as long as your thinking revolves around fear. Once you acknowledge the fear and understand that it's only your thinking that's causing those feelings, the illusion will fall apart, and you'll fall back into peace, joy, and pure love. This is the space you want to stay in, which will allow you to create the positive feelings that are the prerequisite to manifesting all you could possibly imagine for yourself.

CHAPTER 15

CREATING SPACE FOR MIRACLES

"Today I make space for miracles. I recognize that
it's not how big a miracle is that's important, but how
much room I create for it." — Kyle Gray

The Story of the Zen Master and a Scholar - Empty Your Cup

Once upon a time, there was a wise Zen master. People traveled from far away to seek his help. In return, he would teach them and show them the way to enlightenment. On this particular day, a scholar visited the master for advice. *"I have come to ask you to teach me about Zen,"* the scholar said.

Soon, it became obvious that the scholar was full of his own opinions and knowledge. He interrupted the master repeatedly with his own stories and failed to listen to what the master had to say. The master calmly suggested that they should have tea.

So the master gently poured his guest a cup. The cup was filled, yet he kept pouring until the cup overflowed onto the table, onto the floor, and finally onto the scholar's robes. The scholar cried, *"Stop! The cup is full already. Can't you see?"* *"Exactly,"* the Zen master replied with a smile. *"You are like this cup — so full of ideas that nothing more will fit in. Come back to me with an empty cup."*

It is ironic how much could be written about nothing. That's what space is: nothing. When we study the Universe and quantum physics, we realize that everything comes from nothing. Therefore, the great spiritual masters call this The Great Nothingness. For there to be creation, there must first be space. The same is true for our minds. If you want something new to be created, such as new thoughts, you must first create space to receive new ideas that can change your life. Like the teacup, if your mind is completely full of old thinking, it is impossible to have any new thoughts come into your mind to create the change you seek.

The way we can create this space is through non-thinking. When we stop our strenuous efforts to think, we immediately create space where new thoughts and ideas can enter our minds. Questions that challenge our current thinking are also a great way to create space in our minds.

All the magic happens in this space of nothingness. For instance, great athletes go through intense training periods, but the best athletes know that they need an equally intense period of rest afterward to stay in peak performance. It is during this rest period that they recover, build muscle, and become stronger. This space they create for themselves through rest is where everything they want from the workout manifests.

When Thomas Edison was confronted with a particularly challenging problem, he would sleep in his chair while holding a steel ball in each of his hands. Eventually, he would slip into a deep enough stage of sleep where the ball would drop, wake him up, and a solution to his problem would pop into his mind. Everything comes from nothing, and Edison understood this concept of creating space for new thoughts to enter his mind instead of attempting to effort his way into solving problems with his old way of thinking. He knew that old thinking would not give him the solution to his challenges.

"We can't solve problems by using the same level of consciousness we were at when we created them." — Albert Einstein

Einstein had different quirky, enigmatic behaviors like Edison, but a similar understanding of creating space. When Einstein was stuck on a difficult problem, he would stop working on it and play the violin. As he played, the answer would come to him out of seemingly nowhere, and then he'd have the solution to his problem. Einstein had created space within his mind through non-thinking to be able to receive divine insights from the Universe.

We don't have to try to figure everything out. Even the people we deem geniuses didn't strain and effort their way into making the greatest discoveries in the world, so what makes us think that we have to? We are no different from them and connected to the same Source. With the correct understanding, we can also receive insights into any challenge we're facing. We're only ever one thought, one insight, and one idea away from living a completely different experience of life.

Here's the process for receiving divine insights when you're confronted with a challenge:

1. Become aware that your thinking is the root cause of all negative emotions.

2. Create space by surrendering any manual thinking from the personal mind and have complete faith that your intuition (God/Universe/Infinite Intelligence) will give you the answer. Surrender the how and when the answer will come to you.

3. Become aware of any feelings that arise as you surrender and magnify those feelings of love, peace, and joy. Meet what you're facing with love, and the answer will come to you.

If it seems almost too simple, that's a good thing. The truth is always simple. Although it may be simple, it's not always easy, and even the greatest spiritual masters struggle at times. What's important is not when we get caught in our thinking (because it's inevitable) but what we do when we catch ourselves thinking again. As long as you continually remember that we can only ever feel what we're thinking and that thinking is the root cause of our suffering, you're free.

CHAPTER 16

WHAT HAPPENS WHEN YOU BEGIN LIVING IN NON-THINKING (POTENTIAL OBSTACLES)

"Do not let the behavior of others destroy
your inner peace." — Dalai Lama

As you go along your journey of non-thinking, you'll inevitably hit some roadblocks along the way, so I'd like to bring up some of those potential issues before you encounter them so that it is a little bit easier for you.

Once you begin living in a state of non-thinking, it is a deeply peaceful experience of life. Worries, stress, and anxiety seem to vanish before your eyes because when you don't see things as problems anymore, they stop being a problem for you. You'll notice that you haven't felt this type of serenity in your life before, and thus, it will feel unfamiliar.

We as humans biologically don't like what's unfamiliar because it means uncertainty. What's ironic is that right about this time, most people begin thinking that something is wrong because they feel so happy and peaceful the majority of the day. Many feel like they're not as productive, have lost their "edge," or are lazier. This is far from the truth, and it's just your brain attempting to begin thinking again to create the illusion of "safety" it wants to feel. The reality is that we are most productive as humans when we are happy and in a state of non-thinking. Time seems to fly when we are in a state of pure joy. Tasks are easier, we perform better, people gravitate to us, we attract more abundance, and miracles begin to occur out of nowhere. You just have to stay in the state of non-thinking long enough to experience these things, and you'll never want to go back.

This is when faith becomes paramount — having faith that things will be okay. Know that the Universe is working for you, not against you. Everything happens for a reason, and there are no failures in life, just lessons and opportunities for us to grow. We must have faith in the unknown because that's the only place that contains the possibility for anything to be different than the life we're living right now. The unknown is where all possibilities exist, including everything you could ever want for your life. Once you have the courage to make the leap into the unknown and not be afraid of it anymore, it's impossible that your life won't change.

If you begin to feel like something's wrong because you feel way too peaceful and content, know that it's only your mind trying to make you think again. Your mind is the greatest salesman and knows exactly what to say to lure you back into its vicious cycle of destructive thinking. It is in this moment that you have the choice to have faith in the unknown and stay in the feeling of happiness, peace, and love or to go back to the old patterns of familiar pain and psychological suffering. We can either choose to be free and happy in the unknown or to be confined and suffer in the familiar.

If you do fall back into thinking, it is completely okay. Do not beat yourself up about it. Don't feel guilty that it happened. Punishing yourself is unnecessary because that will only perpetuate the thinking. Know that it is human to think. Once you catch yourself and see that your thinking is causing your suffering, that's all you have to do to bring yourself to a state of peace, happiness, and love again. The transition can happen painlessly and effortlessly if you let it.

CHAPTER 17

NOW WHAT?

"There will come a time when you believe everything is finished, and that will be the beginning." — Louis L'Amor

Although this is the end of the book, it is just the beginning of a new life for you. You are only ever one thought away from peace, love, and joy — which come from a state of non-thinking. Remember this and keep it close to your heart because it is all the hope you need when life gets inevitably tough. In the beginning, I promised you that you would not be the same person you were before reading this book. If you began reading this book with the intention of having an open and willing mind, then you have already received numerous insights that have completely changed the way you look at life, and thus, you are not the same person as you were before. Once you see something new from an insight, you cannot unsee it. Once your consciousness expands, it cannot contract again. We may forget from time to time and cause ourselves to suffer when we begin thinking again, but as soon as we remember that, we immediately realize that we are the ever-expanding awareness of life itself and find love, peace, and joy in the present.

If this seems too simple and can't be all there is, it is just your mind causing you to think again. The truth is simple and will always be. Anything that makes something complex and intricate only takes you further from the truth. The truth is not something you think but know and feel deep in your soul. Listen to that still inner wisdom inside you that knows all of this. Let it guide you through your life. We are most fulfilled when we listen to our soul. The world will continuously advertise to us that we are not enough, are missing something, or don't have everything we want. People will constantly bombard you with their own opinions, judgments, and advice. Know that they are innocently caught up in their thinking and thank them for caring, but do not fall into the illusion that you need any of that. Everything you could ever want and need is already inside of you. You are already all the love, joy, peace, and fulfillment you seek. It is only when we forget that fact and get caught up in our thinking that we do not see it.

Continue to live in this state of pure peace and let go of any thinking that may enter your mind. The longer you stay in this space, the more miracles will appear in your life. Although you can go and share this message with every person you meet, you won't even need to because they will notice something completely different about you. You'll be glowing, vibrant, and emanating pure love and joy — and they will begin asking why and how. You are now equipped with everything you need to know on how to stop your own psychological suffering and embody a state of peace, love, and joy, which is always available to you at all times. There's a good chance that you have already experienced the bliss of knowing and being this.

There is no coincidence that you have picked up this book and for us to be able to share our journey here together. I am always amazed at all the divine intercessions that must have happened for us to be together right now. It is truly humbling and an incredible blessing that you have allowed me to guide you through this infinitely beautiful experience we call life.

Before we close this chapter, I have one small favor to ask. If you have found this book helpful or insightful, it would be an honor if you could take 60 seconds to leave a review about this book on Amazon. I would truly love to hear your thoughts, insights, feedback, journey, and everything in between. The few words you share there will help spread this message to so many souls who are also looking for the same answers you are, and it will change someone's life (because who doesn't read Amazon reviews before they buy something, right?).

You may scan the QR code here to leave a short review:

For anyone interested in connecting with me further, I would love to hear from you at hello@josephnguyen.org about your experience. Hearing other people's stories brings me such a deep feeling of joy, so I keep my inbox open for those who want to share. It would be an honor to hear from you.

From My Heart To Yours,

Joseph

P.S. In the next few pages, there will be a summary and guides to help you implement much of what is mentioned in this book.

If you feel inspired and want more from me, I'd love to invite you to visit my website (www.josephnguyen.org), where workshops, courses, and journals are available to help you on your journey. Any new book release will be announced on my website as well.

You may scan the QR code below to visit my website:

My Other Books

Don't Believe Everything You Think: Why Your Thinking Is the Beginning & End of Suffering

Beyond Thoughts: An Exploration of Who We Are Beyond Our Minds

Healing Anxiety & Overthinking Journal & Workbook: Let Go of Anxiety, Overcome Fear, Find Peace & End Suffering

Boundaries = Freedom: How To Create Boundaries That Set You Free Without Feeling Guilty

The Art of Creating: How To Create Art That Transforms Yourself And The World

I also have courses on writing and creativity.

You may find my books and courses on my website at www.josephnguyen.org. My books can also be found on Amazon and many other online sites that sell books.

SUMMARY OF NON-THINKING

- Thinking is the root cause of all suffering.

- There is no other answer to why we feel negative emotions other than that it is from our own thinking. Everything can be traced back to our thinking, which makes problem-solving very simple. Once we realize that our thinking is causing how we feel, we can let go of it and return to our natural state of peace, love, and joy. When we let go of our thinking, it creates space for us to allow all positive emotions we want to feel to surface from within us.

- We don't live in reality; we live in a PERCEPTION of reality, which is created by our own thinking.

- Thinking is NOT an effect of our experiences, but the CAUSE of it.

- The thoughts in our minds are not facts.

- Our thinking only has control over us if we believe it. Let go of the belief in the thought to let go of the suffering.

- Our feelings are direct feedback and an innate internal guidance system to let us know whether we lack understanding or have absolute clarity of truth. Feelings are an invitation to deepen our understanding of the truth.

- We are in flow when we are not thinking.

- There is no separation between us, the Universe, and all of life when we are not thinking. It is only when we think that we cut ourselves from Source and feel separate from all things (the birth of the ego).

- Thinking and thoughts are two different things. Thinking is a verb and is the act of negatively judging the thoughts in our minds, which causes suffering. Thoughts are nouns, which are inherently neutral until we judge them through thinking.

- We think because it is a biological response to survive. Our minds think only because it is trying to keep us alive, but it does not help us thrive. It is only concerned with our safety and survival, not our fulfillment. Thinking holds us back from our Highest Selves by causing negative feelings that prevent us from following our true callings.

- Our minds are limited to our personal experiences. If you want to receive insights, creativity, and knowledge beyond the capabilities of your current self, choose to listen to Infinite Intelligence rather than your finite mind. This infinite source of truth is always available to us if we allow it to be.

- Universal Intelligence/Mind is the energy that is everything in this universe. It is the source of where everything comes from that is before form, and we are made up of it. This energy has a feeling, which is the feeling of love, peace, joy, connection, and well-being. We embody this energy when we let go of our thinking.

- Since we are always connected to the same source of Infinite Intelligence, once we let go of our thinking, we access new thoughts, ideas, and insights, even if we have never experienced them. The more we trust our intuition and this Infinite Intelligence, the more we will receive these insights that are always available.

- Our default states are peace, love, joy, and all positive emotions. Only when we begin thinking are we taken out of that natural state. Once we let go of our thinking, we fall back into our natural state of being and experience all positive feelings effortlessly.

- We are ever only one thought or insight away from expanding our consciousness and experiencing a deeper feeling of love at all times, which comes from a state of non-thinking.

- Clarity is the nature of our minds and our default state. It is only when we get caught up in our thinking that things do not seem so. If we let go of our thinking, we return to our "factory default" setting of peace, love, joy, and a quiet mind.

- Nothing is inherently wrong with anyone or anything in the Universe, but our thinking will make us think so. You do not have to be fixed because you are not broken. There is only something for you to realize and remember: thinking is the root cause of our suffering. You do not have to do anything about your thinking. All you have to do is shift your understanding of thinking, and you will fall back into the truth of who you are, which is beyond your thinking, your body, and everything you think you know. As soon as you let go of your thinking, you become one with Infinite Intelligence, allowing you to feel a never-ending abundance of love, peace, and joy always available to you because that is your true nature.

- When you make space for Infinite Intelligence, it makes space for you. The more you trust it, the more it trusts you. There's never an end to how

much space you can make for it. When you priori-
tize making space in your life and mind for Infinite
Intelligence to come through, your life will change.

- Eliminate or minimize things that may make you more prone to thinking (things that cause you to be in a fight or flight mode).

- Eliminate or minimize as many things and actions in your life that do not inspire you or excite you.

- Create an environment that helps put you into a non-thinking state.

- Create a morning activation ritual to help you start your day in a peaceful, non-thinking state. Use this space to receive insights from Infinite Intelligence to help you navigate life.

- Create space in your day to decompress, relax, and return to a state of non-thinking. Write out things you can do during your day to help you achieve this. It could be journaling, taking a walk, meditating, playing with your pets, taking a nap, doing yoga, or anything relaxing.

Framework For How To Stop Thinking

1. Realize thinking is the root of all suffering (understand the true nature of thinking).

   - Realize if you're suffering, you're thinking.

- Realize the difference between thinking and thoughts.
- Don't try to find the root cause. Thinking is the root cause.

2. Create space for persisting negative thinking
    - Allow them to be there and acknowledge them for what they are.
    - Understand that you are the sacred space that holds these feelings, but that you are not the feelings themselves.
    - Don't be afraid to be alone with your thinking; have the courage to allow it to be in your consciousness. Welcome it in and see that the thinking just wants to be acknowledged.
    - Realize that negative thinking only has power over you if you believe in it.
    - Once you allow them to exist in your consciousness and don't resist the feelings, you can look beyond them to see the truth.
    - Every feeling contains a seed of truth, which will help deepen your awareness and allow you to experience life more fully.

3. Once you acknowledge the thinking, allow it all to pass and allow yourself to just be without attaching to anything. Positive emotions, like peace, love, and

joy, will naturally arise. Allow yourself to enjoy these emotions as they come up. If the negative feeling persists, repeat step one until you've found some peace.

Potential Obstacles

1. Not wanting to let go of thinking because you think it got you to where you are.

   - While this is true, you must realize that what got you here won't get you there. If you want to break the vicious cycle of suffering and the same self-destructive patterns repeating in your life, you'll have to do something different. Insanity is doing the same thing over and over again, but expecting a different result. The real question is, do you want to be at peace or not? If you understand that thinking is the root cause of all of your suffering and do not want to be unhappy any longer, then you will be able to make the leap of faith into non-thinking.

2. Not enough faith

   - For there to even be a possibility that there could be a life filled with joy, peace, and love every single day, you must first believe that it is possible. One must also believe that they are part of something much bigger, which is the life force that has been taking care of them this whole time (the Universe/God). Having faith in something much bigger than we are without being able to fully comprehend it with our finite minds is the only way we can surrender our manual efforts and experience total peace in our lives versus worrying about everything.

3. Fear

- Fear is a completely normal emotion when it comes to trusting in the Universe, which is also the unknown. Fear indicates something is very important to us, which is a great sign. Everything we could ever want is on the other side of fear. The test we must pass to obtain all we desire is fear itself. The way out is through and going deep within yourself to see and know that you will be okay no matter what. This fear cannot and will not kill you, but if you do not confront it, it will take the life of all your dreams instead. Thinking is the root cause of fear. If you don't think, there is no fear. Follow the framework for how to stop thinking to overcome fear and experience what life can be like without limits.

How You Will Know If You're In A State Of Non-Thinking

When you're not thinking, you experience complete peace, love, joy, passion, excitement, inspiration, bliss, and any positive emotion your consciousness can be aware of. You may have thoughts, but you are unattached to them and allow them to flow through you without any friction or pain from thinking. You don't feel any psychological or emotional suffering. You're not thinking about the past or future. They do not matter or exist to you because you're fully in the present moment. You feel like you're in flow. You lose sense of time, space, and even your sense of self. You feel "one" with life. This is how you know you are not thinking.

Reflection Prompts

On a scale of 1-10, how much did you think today? (1 being low, 10 being high)

What percentage of your day was spent in fight or flight mode? What percentage was spent in a relaxed, calm state?

A Guide To Creating A Non-Thinking Environment

Your environment will either induce and support the state of non-thinking, or it can make you more prone to thinking.

Although we create our reality from the inside out, our environment often still affects us. Since we are spiritual beings living in a physical world, we cannot completely detach from this 3D world just yet, so creating an environment conducive to non-thinking is essential. The best way to be productive is to eliminate distractions instead of trying to do more.

Similarly, if we eliminate many things that we know trigger us to relapse back into thinking, we will be able to stay in a peaceful state of non-thinking much more easily. Remember that changing your environment and not yourself will not work long-term. A delicate blend of both will be what you need to create a beautiful life you love to live.

Framework For Removing Thinking Triggers

1. Perform an audit to see what things can make you more susceptible to thinking and make a list.

   A. Write down everything that comes to mind. What can help is to tap into your intuition and feel energetically in your body if this specific thing in your environment will help or hurt you. If you are in a calm, relaxed state, the answer will be obvious.

   B. If you're having trouble coming up with things, remember what tends to put you in a fight or flight mode, make you anxious or overthink. Anything that puts you into a survival state will not help you maintain a state of non-thinking.

   C. If it is still difficult to think of things, you can keep a journal as you go about your week and write down anything that seems to put you into a fight or flight mode. You'll have a nice list by the end of the week.

2. Organize all of the things you wrote down into categories

   A. Here are some examples of categories

      I. Physical Health

a. What things that you put into your body can make you more prone to experience a fight or flight response (anxiety, stress, overthinking)? Foods, stimulants, drinks, etc.

II. Physical Environment

b. What things in your physical environment can make you more prone to experience a fight or flight response (anxiety, stress, overthinking)?

III. Digital Environment

c. What things on your phone, computer, or TV can make you more prone to experience a fight or flight response (anxiety, stress, overthinking)?

IV. Digital Consumption

d. What media/content when you consume can make you more prone to experience a fight or flight response (anxiety, stress, overthinking)?

3. After you categorize everything, reorganize your list and begin ranking the items from things that affect you most to the least.

4. Choose the top items from each list and create an action item on what you plan to do to remove it from your environment. Choose only what would be manageable and possible for you to remove without making you prone to even more stress (this would defeat the purpose of the exercise). Start small, and after you've become acquainted with the changes and seen the impact, you can begin eliminating other things.

Framework For Creating A Non-Thinking Environment

Write down all of the things that help you get into a relaxed, peaceful, non-thinking state. These can be things like exercise, meditation, having a certain genre of music on, location, etc.

Organize the items on your list into categories.

1. Examples Of Categories
    I. Physical Health
        a. What things you put into your body help you feel healthy, sustainably energized, and peaceful?
    II. Physical Environment
        a. What things in your physical environment help you feel aligned with your divine self?
    III. Digital Environment
        a. What things on your phone, computer, or TV help you to feel aligned with your divine self?
    IV. Digital Consumption
        a. What media/content do you consume that helps you feel aligned with your highest self?

2. Rank the items in each category from most impactful to least impactful to help you get into and remain in a non-thinking state.

3. Choose the top items from each list and create an action item on how you will incorporate it into your life. Try not to do too much at once because it can be overwhelming. Do what is manageable for you for now, and you can add on more later after you've become acquainted with it.

4. Create an activation ritual or morning routine that helps you get into a state of non-thinking and enables you to align with your highest self. Plan out your ideal morning routine that you can do now. Start small, and don't overwhelm yourself. Ensure you have time to create space (like meditation, yoga, or any similar spiritual practice to help you tune into Infinite Intelligence).

5. How you start your day will create momentum for how your day will go. If you start your day by checking your phone, emails, and what you have to do, you're starting your day in a stressful, fight-or-flight mode of thinking, which will carry on for the rest of the day.

6. Suppose you begin your day in a peaceful state and perform a routine that gets you into a state of non-

thinking. In that case, you will carry that momentum throughout your day, and it will be much harder to get caught up in external things that could make you relapse into thinking and stress. This is why all the greatest spiritual masters have morning rituals or routines.

Framework For Implementing Non-Thinking Into Your Work

1. Create a list of things you do in your work that drain you of energy — things that you don't like doing or feel overall heavy in your work.

2. Create a list of things you do in your work that give you energy — things that make you feel inspired, energetic, alive, and light.

3. Go back through your whole list and give a rating for each activity that you do on a scale from 1-10 with 1 being extremely energy draining and 10 making you feel the most alive and inspired when you do it.

4. Each week, eliminate 1-3 things from your energy-draining list and do more of the activities that are a 9 and 10 on your list.

5. The goal is to get to a point where you're spending 80% of your work time doing things that are a 9 and 10 on your list.

A Guide To Overcoming Destructive Habits/Behaviors

As you create more space and begin not thinking as much, you'll quickly discover that you will become aware of a lot of negative, destructive habits you may have that keep making you more prone to suffering. This is completely okay. Please do not beat yourself up because it will only worsen things. Here is a more detailed guide below that will help you break any destructive habits:

1. Become aware of what behavior you want to change and confirm that you genuinely want to alter it. Understand that if you want to change and stop the vicious cycle of suffering, you will have to change and let go of the beliefs you're holding onto that are creating the suffering. If you don't want to change it, there's no point in continuing forward, but if you do want to change, let's begin the process of letting go.

2. Write down in exact, meticulous detail what happens with this behavior (how many times it happens, when it happens, etc.) Don't spare any details.

3. What are you feeling in the moment right before you begin the behavior? What's the feeling that triggers the behavior? Be honest with yourself.

4. What specific thinking patterns are going on? **What are you saying to yourself in the moment when this happens?** Describe it in exact detail.

5. What beliefs do you have about this habit? What conclusions have you made that compel you to feel like you **HAVE** to perform this behavior/action?

6. How do you feel when you believe that thinking?

7. What do you believe will happen if you don't perform the behavior? In other words, what consequences do you believe will happen if you don't perform the action?

8. Is it ABSOLUTELY 100% true that it will happen if you don't perform the behavior?

9. Can you see how destructive this thinking is and how much it causes you to suffer?

10. Are you willing to let this thinking and behavior go now?

11. Consult your inner wisdom and highest self. What is it trying to tell you? What is it trying to help you learn? How is it telling you to restore balance in your life? How is it telling you to grow right now? Create space and wait for an insight from Infinite Intelligence as to why you actually want to change.

12. When you receive the insight, allow yourself to fully feel the freedom, peace, and joy. Feel the

weight lifted off your shoulders. You'll know you did it right if you physically and energetically feel lighter and don't see the action/habit in the same way anymore. Fully immerse yourself in the feeling of deep gratitude and just allow yourself to be.

13. Write down any insight you've had and journal your experience so you can have documentation of these miracles in your life.

What To Do If The Feeling Comes Back Up Again

Follow this guide again until you have an insight or breakthrough that completely changes how you look at life.

ACKNOWLEDGEMENT

Thank you, Sydney Banks, for sharing the principles you have discovered with the world. Because of you, I have found the truth within myself and now have the same privilege of sharing it with the world.

Thank you to my teachers and mentors, Joe Bailey and Michael Neill, for sharing the Three Principles with me, which have changed my life forever. I am eternally grateful for your generosity and heart of service that keeps giving. Thank you for all you do and will continue to do for others. Thank you to all my dear friends and family (Mom, Dad, Anthony, James, Christian, Bryan, and many more) for helping me discover my divinity and encouraging me to write this book. Without any of you, this book would not be in existence. Please know that because of you, the impact you have on me and anyone who will ever come across this book is infinite and will continue to change the lives of generations yet to be born.

Thank you, Kenna, for being one of the loveliest, effervescent souls I have ever experienced and for showing me what true unconditional love is. Your beautiful presence perpetually humbles me, and I can never thank you enough for the gift of your never-ending love for me and everyone you meet.

30521324R00076